MW01141229

# PASSION WEEK EXPERIENCE

*Written by*
Kelly Wehunt & Chad Balthrop

*Produced by*
Brad Aylor

**First Baptist Church of Owasso**

*Passion Week Experience*
Copyright © 2018 by First Baptist Church of Owasso
ISBN 978-1-329-92731-5

Published by First Baptist Church of Owasso
PO BOX 1020
Owasso, OK 74055
(918) 272-2294 | fbcowasso.org

All Scripture quotations, unless otherwise indicated, are taken from the Holy
Bible, New King James Version. Copyright © 1982.

*"For He made Him who knew no sin to be sin for us, that we might become the righteousness of God in Him."*

*2 Corinthians 5:21*

# CONTENTS

# WELCOME TO THE PASSION WEEK EXPERIENCE

No single individual has had more influence on the history of the world than Jesus Christ. For generations, His life and teaching have transformed individuals and communities. Our modern view of freedom, civil rights, generosity, compassion, and humility are the direct result of His influence. The message of the cross is so compelling that even skeptics find themselves living in a cruciform shaped culture.

Before Jesus, generosity was something practiced between family, friends, or your community. After Jesus, we hear the challenge to love our enemies and our neighbors as ourselves.

Before Jesus, the weak, widowed, poor, and orphaned were cast aside. After Jesus, our attention is turned to their care.

Whether you realize it or not, the way you think is shaped by the life of this man, Jesus.

It's a life worth knowing.

You are about to take part in an interactive experience through the stations of the cross. You will discover the events that led to the death, burial, and resurrection of Jesus Christ.

This modern approach to an ancient practice will connect you with the most significant moment in history. Each station will immerse you in an environment that enables you to experience the meaning and emotion of that time.

This book will be your guide.

At each station, you will be able to pause, read, reflect, and interact with the elements of that moment.

 SCRIPTURE - Read the passage of Scripture that reveals the history and spiritual significance of the events and elements of that station.

 EXPLANATION - Discover the historical and scriptural context of the station and it's relevance to you.

 INVITATION - Interact with each station according to the instructions.

 WITH YOUR FAMILY - With young children, consider each question and discuss a simplified explanation of the station.

 PRAYER - These prayers are a suggested starting point as you turn your heart and mind to God.

As your journey begins, we are praying for you. Our prayers are best expressed through scripture.

*"And this I pray, that your love may abound still more and more in knowledge and all discernment, that you may approve the things that are excellent, that you may be sincere and without offense till the day of Christ, being filled with the fruits of righteousness which are by Jesus Christ, to the glory and praise of God."*

*Philippians 1:9-11*

PREPARE YOUR HEART

# SCRIPTURE

## ROMANS 3:10-20

As it is written:
> There is none righteous, no, not one;
> There is none who understands;
> There is none who seeks after God.
> They have all turned aside;
> They have together become unprofitable;
> There is none who does good, no, not one.

> Their throat is an open tomb;
> With their tongues they have practiced deceit;
> The poison of asps is under their lips;
> Whose mouth is full of cursing and bitterness.

> Their feet are swift to shed blood;
> Destruction and misery are in their ways;
> And the way of peace they have not known.

> There is no fear of God before their eyes.

Now we know that whatever the law says, it says to those who are under the law, that every mouth may be stopped, and all the world may become guilty before God. Therefore, by the deeds of the law no flesh will be justified in His sight, for by the law is the knowledge of sin.

## PSALM 24:3-5

> Who may ascend into the hill of the Lord?
> Or who may stand in His holy place?
> He who has clean hands and a pure heart,
> Who has not lifted up his soul to an idol,
> Nor sworn deceitfully.
> He shall receive blessing from the Lord,
> And righteousness from the God of his salvation.

 ## EXPLANATION

None is righteous. No one understands. No one seeks God. In this age, it's easy to think highly of ourselves. It's easy to look at our accomplishments and allow pride to creep in. It's easy to forget the magnitude of what Jesus has done for us. Read Romans 3:10-20 one more time. Take your time.

These are harsh words, harsh words about you and me.

These words describe us before we come to know Christ.

Romans 3 highlights one significant truth:

*We are all wicked and completely lost without Christ.*

The Old Testament is full of stories about the depravity of humanity. The stories of the Old Testament show how God's people turn away from Him to chase their own selfish desires. This choice only leads to destruction. Old Testament Law describes the rituals, rules, and sacrifices God's people tried to follow. They believed following these rules would reconcile them to God. But the Law revealed our absolute inability to redeem ourselves from sin. This sin, the wrongs you have done, separates you from God and keeps you from having a relationship with Him.

Sin is a disease we all suffer. There aren't enough good works you can do to cure yourself.

# INVITATION

Take a few moments to consider the weight of your sin.

In the Old Testament, priests washed their hands as a way to prepare for religious acts. This hand washing was a symbolic act of purity.

Approach the table to participate in a symbolic "washing of the hands" as a way to spiritually prepare your heart.

# WITH YOUR FAMILY

Ask your children to think about a meal you eat at home. What do we ask you to do before we eat?

Wash your hands.

Why? Because they need to be clean. The Bible tells us that having sin in our lives is like having dirty hands. Explain that sin is any wrong thing we do. What we're about to do together will help us see what Jesus went through so that we could be forgiven. We don't deserve what Jesus did for us, but because of His sacrifice, we can be forgiven of our sin. It's like being given clean hands and a pure heart. Receiving this forgiveness is life changing!

# PRAYER

Father,

It is easy to get caught up in the busyness of the Easter season and forget the magnitude of what You did for me. Help me to clear my mind and feel the weight of my sin as I walk through this experience. Remind me that without You, I am nothing.

Let me see my sin. Grant me the gift of repentance. Give me the strength to turn from my sin and the faith to trust You alone. Thank You for what You are about to show me and for walking through this experience with me.

In Jesus' name I pray. Amen.

SERVING HE PROVIDES, BODY BROKEN FOR US.

## SCRIPTURE

### MATTHEW 26:26-29

> And as they were eating, Jesus took bread, blessed and broke it, and gave it to the disciples and said, "Take, eat; this is My body."

> Then He took the cup, gave thanks, and gave it to them, saying, "Drink from it, all of you. For this is My blood of the new covenant, which is shed for many for the remission of sins. But I say to you, I will not drink of this fruit of the vine from now on until that day when I drink it new with you in My Father's kingdom."

## EXPLANATION

Jesus, like most Jewish people of that time, understood something important about sin. The only way to be cleansed of sin was through sacrifice.

In the Old Testament, it was necessary to sacrifice crops and livestock to be made right before God. Yet, these things only provided a temporary solution. It was an exhausting, painful, bloody act that had to occur over and over and over again. The prophets of scripture pointed to a perfect sacrifice. One day this sacrifice would free God's people from the bondage of sin forever.

It was the night of the Passover Celebration. Jesus would celebrate His last meal with His disciples. He told them of the sacrifice He would make for the world. He used bread to illustrate how His body would be broken for us. He used wine to illustrate how His blood would be spilled for us.

It would be horrific and painful. But Jesus knew it was the only way to save us from our sin.

## INVITATION

Jesus explained to the disciples what was about to happen. He used the matzah bread of the Passover Meal to help them understand. Folded in the napkin on the table were three pieces of matzah. The top, a symbol of God. The bottom, a symbol of humanity. The middle, a symbol of the High Priest who connects humanity with God.

It was from the center that Jesus took the matzah, broke, and shared it with His disciples. The symbolism was clear. Jesus is the High Priest who forever connects His people with God.

Taste the matzah bread of the Seder as you reflect on the reality of that day.

Jesus had spent three and a half years preparing His disciples for these next moments. Yet they still didn't understand.

Isn't that like us?

You may have heard the story many times and still not understand how momentous it is that Jesus gave His life for us. You don't deserve it. None of us do. Yet God's love for you is deeper than you can imagine. His gift to you through His Son, is more gracious than words can express.

The small bowl and towel are a reminder that this was an evening filled with surprises. John 13 describes the scene before dinner. Jesus knelt down like the lowliest of servants to wash the disciple's feet.

Why would the King of Kings, God Himself, do such a thing? To teach us that just as He loves us, we should love and serve others.

 # WITH YOUR FAMILY

Discuss with your family.

Jesus used food to help His friends understand what He was about to do for them. He shared bread to represent how His body would be broken on the cross. He shared wine to represent His blood that He would shed for us. Jesus wants us to understand, remember, and appreciate what He did for us. He also wants us to serve others.

 # PRAYER

Jesus,

Help me to see the importance of what You did for me on the cross that week. Don't let me miss it. Help me to love others the way You love me. Thank You that You love me even though I don't deserve it. Help me to do the same for others. Remind me daily of my absolute need for You. Out of thankfulness, help me to live my life for You.

In Jesus' name. Amen.

# THE
# PASSION
# WEEK
# EXPERIENCE

SUBMISSION: NOT MY WILL, BUT YOURS.

 ## SCRIPTURE

### MATTHEW 26:36-46

Then Jesus came with them to a place called Gethsemane, and said to the disciples, "Sit here while I go and pray over there." And He took with Him Peter and the two sons of Zebedee, and He began to be sorrowful and deeply distressed. Then He said to them, "My soul is exceedingly sorrowful, even to death. Stay here and watch with Me."

He went a little farther and fell on His face, and prayed, saying, "O My Father, if it is possible, let this cup pass from Me; nevertheless, not as I will, but as You will."

Then He came to the disciples and found them sleeping, and said to Peter, "What! Could you not watch with Me one hour? Watch and pray, lest you enter into temptation. The spirit indeed is willing, but the flesh is weak."

Again, a second time, He went away and prayed, saying, "O My Father, if this cup cannot pass away from Me unless I drink it, Your will be done." And He came and found them asleep again, for their eyes were heavy.

So He left them, went away again, and prayed the third time, saying the same words. Then He came to His disciples and said to them, "Are you still sleeping and resting? Behold, the hour is at hand, and the Son of Man is being betrayed into the hands of sinners. Rise, let us be going. See, My betrayer is at hand."

## EXPLANATION

Submission is a word that evokes a variety of different feelings. At its most basic, submission is allowing someone else to take the lead for the decisions in your life. The Bible tells us, as Christians, we are to submit to Christ in all we do. This scene in the garden is a beautiful picture of how Christ Himself lived in submission to God, the Father. Jesus knew the pain He would experience on the cross. He also knew, at any moment, He could walk away from it.

But He didn't.

Instead, Jesus submitted to God's plan. Hebrews 12:1-2 tell us Jesus submitted to God, "...for the joy set before Him." Jesus knew God's plan was the only way you could be forgiven. He submitted to God. He endured the pain of the cross for the joy set before Him. What was that joy?

That joy was you.

Out of love for you and honor for God, Jesus submitted to God's plan and turned to face the reality of what He had to do next.

## INVITATION

Be still.

Immerse yourself in the peace of the garden. In contrast to the peace, consider the anguish Jesus experienced as He prayed. Jesus faced a decision that we face every day of our lives.

Will I submit to God even when it's hard or painful?

Will I turn and walk my own way?

Consider the decisions or hardships you face. Will you choose to submit to and trust God?

# WITH YOUR FAMILY

Ask your children.

What is something we have asked you to do that is really hard? (Examples: Clean your room, go to bed, be nice to your sister, etc.)

Sometimes it's hard because you just don't want to do it. When you choose to do what we ask, you show that you love and trust us.

Jesus knew that dying on the cross would be hard. He also knew what His Father, God, needed Him to do in order to save us. In the garden, He told God He would trust Him and do what needed to be done. I am so thankful He did!

# PRAYER

Jesus,

Thank You for choosing to submit even though it was hard and it hurt. Thank You for choosing to submit for the joy set before you. Sometimes it's hard to believe I am that joy. Thank You for choosing to submit so that I can be forgiven.

It's easy for me to forget to submit to You in the seemingly small things. Out of gratitude to You, help me to trust You with the challenges I face.

In Your name I pray. Amen.

# THE
# PASSION
# WEEK
# EXPERIENCE

BETRAYAL. WHEN WE TRADE SOMETHING CHEAP FOR HIM.

 ## SCRIPTURE

### MATTHEW 26:14-25

Then one of the twelve, called Judas Iscariot, went to the chief priests and said, "What are you willing to give me if I deliver Him to you?" And they counted out to him thirty pieces of silver. So from that time he sought opportunity to betray Him.

Now on the first day of the Feast of Unleavened Bread the disciples came to Jesus, saying to Him, "Where do You want us to prepare for You to eat the Passover?"

And He said, "Go into the city to a certain man, and say to him, 'The Teacher says, "My time is at hand; I will keep the Passover at your house with My disciples."'"

So the disciples did as Jesus had directed them; and they prepared the Passover.

When evening had come, He sat down with the twelve. Now as they were eating, He said, "Assuredly, I say to you, one of you will betray Me."

And they were exceedingly sorrowful, and each of them began to say to Him, "Lord, is it I?"

He answered and said, "He who dipped his hand with Me in the dish will betray Me. The Son of Man indeed goes just as it is written of Him, but woe to that man by whom the Son of Man is betrayed! It would have been good for that man if he had not been born."

Then Judas, who was betraying Him, answered and said,

"Rabbi, is it I?"

He said to him, "You have said it."

 ## EXPLANATION

Judas was called by Jesus to be one of the twelve disciples. He knew Jesus. He traveled with Him. Judas saw the miracles and heard the words. He saw the prophecy fulfilled about the coming Messiah. And yet, he traded it all for thirty pieces of silver (Matthew 26:14-16).

You may read this passage with disbelief. How could he? How could a man so close to our Savior be so willing to betray Him for a few weeks worth of salary?

Here you must pause and think. What cheap things do you crave in exchange for Jesus?

"Lord, if You will just give me _____, then I will follow You."

"Father, I know this is wrong, but I don't want to get rid of it. Not even for You."

Before long we find ourselves standing in the place of Judas. We are willing to trade the promises of our Savior for something cheap and meaningless.

 ## INVITATION

Touch the pieces of silver. Hold them in your hand. Examine

the detailed engraving and feel the cold touch of the metal. As you do, ask God to show you the cheap and meaningless things you trade for His life. Ask God to protect you from temptation and to change your appetite for sin. What steps do you need to take today to exchange the cheap and meaningless for the glorious and eternal?

 # WITH YOUR FAMILY

Ask this question.

What is your favorite snack? What is your least favorite snack?

What if I offered to give you your favorite snack? It would seem silly if you chose to eat your least favorite snack instead. Wouldn't it?

Judas was a man who knew Jesus and His teachings. But Judas didn't trust Jesus to give him what he needed. Instead, Judas sold his friendship with Jesus for a small amount of money. Judas betrayed Jesus.

Jesus wants us to choose the best. When we trust Jesus to be the boss of our lives, we choose His best.

 # PRAYER

Father,

I confess. I often exchange Your presence in my life for something cheap and meaningless. Help me to identify the things I focus on more than You. Help me know how to release those things. Thank You for loving me in spite of my willing betrayal of You over and over again.

In Jesus' name. Amen.

# THE

# PASSION
# WEEK
## EXPERIENCE

CRAFTED BY OUR SIN. USED BY OUR SAVIOR.

## SCRIPTURE

### MATTHEW 27:27-31

> Then the soldiers of the governor took Jesus into the Praetorium and gathered the whole garrison around Him. And they stripped Him and put a scarlet robe on Him. When they had twisted a crown of thorns, they put it on His head, and a reed in His right hand. And they bowed the knee before Him and mocked Him, saying, "Hail, King of the Jews!" Then they spat on Him, and took the reed and struck Him on the head. And when they had mocked Him, they took the robe off Him, put His own clothes on Him, and led Him away to be crucified.

## EXPLANATION

Jesus was betrayed, beaten, and mocked. The same people He came to save are the ones who now stare Him in the face and make fun of Him. The torment would only continue to grow stronger and more horrific from here.

Have you ever been wrongfully accused? Have you experienced the affects of lies told about you? Have you carried the burden or received the punishment for someone else's wrong choices?

Jesus willingly suffered the lies, accusations, and punishment for sins He would never commit. Philippians 2:5-11 tells us He chose this torment and torture to take our place.

He gave up His authority as God to become a man.

He gave up His rights as a man to become a servant, a slave, to others.

He gave up His reputation, to be accused of crimes He didn't commit.

He gave up His life, to receive the punishment we so richly deserve.

Through every beating, every mockery, and every ounce of pain, Jesus remained faithful. He was called to save sick, sinful, undeserving people like us from the destruction of sin.

 ## INVITATION

Be careful as you touch the crown of thorns. Pick up the nails. Let the sting of the thorns remind you of the sting of death. Consider the weight of the nails as you consider the weight of your sin. Jesus suffered all these things in your place.

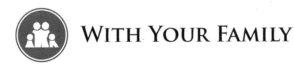 ## WITH YOUR FAMILY

Discuss this with your children.

There are few deaths more painful than death on a cross. Jesus was not only beaten and nailed to the cross. He was made fun of by the people He loved and came to save.

They jammed a crown made of thorns on His head. They drove

huge nails into His hands and feet to hang Him on a cross.

I know this is scary. It's important to understand how much He loves us and all He was willing to go through for us. Even though we don't deserve it.

 **PRAYER**

Jesus,

Thank You for enduring the pain of the beatings, mocking, and the cross for me. I don't deserve the gift You have given me. Help me to love others the way You loved me that day. Give me the courage and strength to love people who reject and ridicule me. I love You.

In Jesus' name. Amen.

# THE
# PASSION
# WEEK
## EXPERIENCE

THE PRICE HE PAID.

## SCRIPTURE

### MATTHEW 27:32-44

Now as they came out, they found a man of Cyrene, Simon by name. Him they compelled to bear His cross. And when they had come to a place called Golgotha, that is to say, Place of a Skull, they gave Him sour wine mingled with gall to drink. But when He had tasted it, He would not drink.

Then they crucified Him, and divided His garments, casting lots, that it might be fulfilled which was spoken by the prophet:

"They divided My garments among them,

And for My clothing they cast lots."

Sitting down, they kept watch over Him there. And they put up over His head the accusation written against Him:

THIS IS JESUS THE KING OF THE JEWS.

Then two robbers were crucified with Him, one on the right and another on the left.

And those who passed by blasphemed Him, wagging their heads and saying, "You who destroy the temple and build it in three days, save Yourself! If You are the Son of God, come down from the cross."

Likewise the chief priests also, mocking with the scribes and elders, said, "He saved others; Himself He cannot save. If He is the King of Israel, let Him now come down from the cross, and we will believe Him. He trusted in God; let Him deliver Him now if He will have Him; for He said, 'I am the Son of God.'"

Even the robbers who were crucified with Him reviled Him with the same thing.

 ## EXPLANATION

They made Him carry His cross.

The path they took was named the Via Dolorosa. "The Way of Suffering". Beaten and bloody. His strength shattered. The Roman soldiers conscripted a man from the crowd, Simon, the Cyrene, to carry the cross for Jesus. All the way to Golgotha. The place of the skull. The name, a reflection of the image people saw every time they looked toward that dreaded hillside.

Right hand and left. Feet laid on those beams. Splinters from the wood digging deeper into the bloody mess of a back already shredded by the whip. A soldier brings a nail. The hammer finds it's mark.

Crack.

Crack.

Crack.

The sound splits the afternoon air. It's the sound of freedom falling. The terrible music of redemption for you and me.

Mocked by the crowd. Abused by the soldiers. Ridiculed by a thief and immersed in the excruciating pain of a torturous death. These would not compare to the agony yet to come. The spotless Son of God would, for the first time in eternity, take into Himself the weight of our sin.

His righteousness removed and made ready for you and me. Like the bitter cold of winter's night, our sin saturates every measure of His existence. All He was. All He is.

And God the Father turns His back on His Son.

# INVITATION

If you choose, a volunteer will help place a crossbeam on your back. Let the weight on your shoulders remind you of the weight of your sin. Walk carefully down the way of suffering. With each step, consider the steps of Jesus. Remember the beating, the mocking, the torture. Remember the righteousness removed, replaced by your sin.

# WITH YOUR FAMILY

Consider this with your family.

Have you ever been so tired you couldn't take another step? Have you been so exhausted you felt like you couldn't lift your arms?

Jesus was beaten so badly He couldn't carry His own cross. A man named Simon was forced to carry it for Him. Jesus walked a long path up the hill to where He would die.

No one forced Him to do it.

He could have stopped it. He could have called angels to take Him away at any moment. But He chose to do it because it was the only way your sins could be forgiven. This is how much He loves you.

# PRAYER

Jesus,

I can't imagine what it is that You did for me that day. I know that God is perfect, and I am not. I know on my own I am lost. Thank You for the deep love you have for me. Thank You that You became sin, who knew no sin, that we might become Your righteousness. Thank You for humbling Yourself to carry Your cross. Your love is amazing. I love You.

In Your name I pray. Amen.

UNRESTRICTED ACCESS.

## SCRIPTURE

### MATTHEW 27:45-51

> Now from the sixth hour until the ninth hour there was darkness over all the land. And about the ninth hour Jesus cried out with a loud voice, saying, "Eli, Eli, lama sabachthani?" that is, "My God, My God, why have You forsaken Me?" Some of those who stood there, when they heard that, said, "This Man is calling for Elijah!" Immediately one of them ran and took a sponge, filled it with sour wine and put it on a reed, and offered it to Him to drink.

> The rest said, "Let Him alone; let us see if Elijah will come to save Him."

> And Jesus cried out again with a loud voice, and yielded up His spirit.

> Then, behold, the veil of the temple was torn in two from top to bottom; and the earth quaked, and the rocks were split...

## EXPLANATION

It began with Adam. The sin that separates us from God.

Yet God's love for us is deep. His passion for us compels Him to make a way to put right what once went wrong.

In the Old Testament, our separation from God was manifest in the construction of the Temple. All could worship from the

Outer Courts. Only Jewish men could worship from the Inner Courts. And only Jewish priests from the appropriate tribe could worship in the Holy Place. Each location represented a closer, more intimate relationship with God. Each location included some, and excluded others. But there was one more room. Only one person had permission to enter this room, and then, only one day per year, the Day of Atonement. The High Priest would step through the curtain to the Holy of Holies and into the presence of God.

Scripture tells us that without the shedding of blood there is no forgiveness of sin. On this day, the High Priest would offer a blood sacrifice atop the Ark of the Covenant, on the Mercy Seat, to atone for the sins of the people of Israel. Without forgiveness, the High Priest would perish as would the nation of Israel. But the blood of this sacrifice was only a lamb. A temporary symbol of the permanent payment Jesus would one day give for all who trust in Him.

Jesus is the Lamb of God who takes away the sin of the world. With the unbearable pain of the cross and the unimaginable weight of our sin, Jesus cries out, "My God, my God, why have You forsaken Me?"

He breathes His last and gives His life in exchange for ours.

With that, forgiveness is available because God is near. The curtain that covers the Holy of Holies is torn from top to bottom. No longer is there any separation. No longer do we need the imperfect and impermanent blood of animals. No longer do priests, people, or places stand between us and God.

Jesus is dead. The curtain is torn. God draws near.

# INVITATION

Approach the Holy of Holies as though you would approach God. Not because this place is holy, but the One represented here is.

Outside the temple, imagine what living outside the presence of God must feel like. Your sin defines you. Because you are not holy you can never be in the presence of God. But God's love for you is deep. His passion for you compels Him to put right what once went wrong. Jesus died in your place.

As you enter the Holy of Holies and view the Ark of the Covenant and the Mercy Seat, recognize the miracle done on your behalf. You are free from sin by the blood of the Lamb. Sin no longer defines you. You don't have to live by the world's rules anymore. Instead, you can boldly enter the Throne Room of the presence of God. You enter, not on the basis of your ability, but in humble recognition of the grace of God given to you.

As you pass through the Holy of Holies, acknowledge the work of the Holy Spirit in your life. The presence of God, once located in the Holy of Holies, now indwells people through His Holy Spirit.

God is with us. Near us. In us.

# WITH YOUR FAMILY

Ask your family.

What words would someone use to describe you?

Would they use your name, describe your appearance, or talk about the things you do?

The Bible uses a word to describe us.

Sinful.

Sin is any wrong thing we do. The Bible tells us that if Jesus isn't the boss of your life, then sin defines you. This is a problem. God won't have anything to do with sin. Sin keeps us from having a right relationship with God.

Do you see this curtain? In ancient times, people believed God lived on the other side of a curtain like this. This curtain blocked people from entering God's presence. Just like your sin keeps you from having a right relationship with God.

Notice the tear in the curtain. It starts at the top and goes all the way to the bottom. On the day Jesus died, this curtain tore from top to bottom. Your way is no longer blocked. Now you can live in the presence of God.

Jesus can forgive your sin. When He does, you are no longer defined by sin. You are now a child of God.

 ## PRAYER

Father,

I am so unworthy. I deserve the death Your son, Jesus, endured. There is no way I could enter Your presence without this incredible sacrifice. Thank You for tearing the curtain and allowing me to have a relationship with You through Jesus.

In Jesus' name. Amen.

WHAT CAN WE OFFER?

## SCRIPTURE

### MATTHEW 27:57-61

> Now when evening had come, there came a rich man from
> Arimathea, named Joseph, who himself had also become a
> disciple of Jesus. This man went to Pilate and asked for the
> body of Jesus. Then Pilate commanded the body to be given
> to him. When Joseph had taken the body, he wrapped it in a
> clean linen cloth, and laid it in his new tomb which he had
> hewn out of the rock; and he rolled a large stone against the
> door of the tomb, and departed. And Mary Magdalene was
> there, and the other Mary, sitting opposite the tomb.

 ## EXPLANATION

Jesus was dead. Darkness covered the city. Was this it? Was
it over? While Jesus' followers scattered, one had the courage
to care for His body. Joseph of Arimathea gave Jesus a proper
burial. One worthy of a king. John 19 gives greater detail.
According to Jewish custom, they prepared the body for burial
using linen and spices.

Joseph laid the body of Jesus in a new tomb, hewn out of
the rock. They rolled a large stone against the door under the
watchful and loving eyes of Mary and Mary Magdalene.

## Invitation

Touch the linen. Smell the spices. What must have been going through the minds of His followers? The man they watched bring the dead to life was now dead Himself. They believed He was Messiah, but this wasn't what they expected. Scared and scattered, they wondered what would happen next.

Some kept the faith. They buried Jesus with the best they had. Matthew 26:1-13 tells the story of a woman who worshiped at the feet of Jesus. She anointed Him with costly oils. Jesus said she did this in anticipation of His burial.

What will it look like for you to give your first and your best for Him?

## With Your Family

Discuss this.

What do we do with someone's body after they die?

We have a funeral.

Even though, for His followers, Jesus' death was sad and scary, one of His followers took the time to bury Jesus. It was expensive. But this follower of Jesus believed Jesus was worthy of a King's burial. He gave Jesus his best.

How can we give Jesus our best every day?

# PRAYER

Father,

Thank You for all you have done for me. I want to give You my first and best every day. There are times I can't see the end when I don't understand the path. There are times when life is difficult and I can't explain Your plan or purpose. Give me hope when all seems lost. Give me faith when things seem hopeless. Don't let my heart be scared or scattered. Instead, let me stand firm in the knowledge that I serve a living Savior. Thank You for Your relentless love for me.

In Jesus' name. Amen.

# — THE —
# PASSION
# WEEK
# EXPERIENCE

# OUR CROSS

S8

WHAT DO WE DO NOW?

## SCRIPTURE

### ROMANS 3:21-28

But now the righteousness of God apart from the law is revealed, being witnessed by the Law and the Prophets, even the righteousness of God, through faith in Jesus Christ, to all and on all who believe. For there is no difference; for all have sinned and fall short of the glory of God, being justified freely by His grace through the redemption that is in Christ Jesus, whom God set forth as a propitiation by His blood, through faith, to demonstrate His righteousness, because in His forbearance God had passed over the sins that were previously committed, to demonstrate at the present time His righteousness, that He might be just and the justifier of the one who has faith in Jesus.

Where is boasting then? It is excluded. By what law? Of works? No, but by the law of faith. Therefore we conclude that a man is justified by faith apart from the deeds of the law.

## EXPLANATION

What will you do with what you've just experienced?

Romans 3 is true for you. You are a sinner. Jesus made a way for you to be forgiven. Without Christ, you are unworthy, unrighteous, and unwilling to seek after God. With Christ, you are forgiven and free. It's a brand new day. His faithfulness is new every morning.

 ## INVITATION

Before participating in this station, answer this question.

Is Jesus Lord of my life?

Have you placed your faith in Him to repent of your sin and receive the incredible gift of His forgiveness? If needed, volunteers and Pastors are available to answer questions and pray with you.

As a believer, take time at this station to pray about the sin that currently weighs you down. Write this temptation or sin on a piece of paper and nail it to the cross. This symbolic act demonstrates your desire to submit to God. As you surrender your will to His, you will become more aware of how much damage sin does to your life.

Nailing this paper to the cross isn't sacred. Everything you've experienced today reveals the truth that none of us are righteous. Nothing you can do will earn your way into a right relationship with God. The sacrifice Jesus made on the cross at Calvary made the way for you to be forgiven and free from sin.

1 John 1:9 says, "If we confess our sins, He is faithful and just to forgive us our sins and to cleanse us from all unrighteousness."

Will you surrender your life today?

# WITH YOUR FAMILY

Parents, this is a great time to talk with your kids about what it means to trust Jesus to forgive our sin. Here are some ways you can know your child is ready to place their faith in Christ.

- When they understand they are a sinner because of the wrong things they have done.

- When they understand that Jesus died on the cross and rose from the dead so they can be forgiven.

- When they are ready to submit to God to be the boss of their life.

Volunteers are available, if you need help talking about this with your child.

Your child may have already placed their faith in Christ. Explain that forgiven people still struggle with sin.

Tell them, "1 John 1:9 says, 'If we confess our sins, He is faithful and just to forgive our sins and to cleanse us from all unrighteousness.'"

This means when we ask Jesus to forgive us, He does.

Pray with them about a specific sin they know they need to ask Jesus to forgive. Ask God to give them the strength and courage to overcome that temptation.

As a symbol of their forgiveness, encourage them to write that sin on a piece of paper and help them nail it to the cross.

 **PRAYER**

Father,

Because I am thankful for what You have done for me, I confess this sin and give it to You. Protect me from temptation. Replace my appetite for sin with a hunger and thirst for righteousness. I know that You can break the chains sin has created in my life. I praise You that this sin no longer has power over me because of Jesus' sacrifice on the cross. Help me to live a life that honors You and encourages others to do the same.

In Jesus' name. Amen.

IN REMEMBRANCE OF ME.

##  SCRIPTURE

### 1 CORINTHIANS 11:23-26

For I received from the Lord that which I also delivered to you: that the Lord Jesus on the same night in which He was betrayed took bread; and when He had given thanks, He broke it and said, "Take, eat; this is My body which is broken for you; do this in remembrance of Me." In the same manner He also took the cup after supper, saying, "This cup is the new covenant in My blood. This do, as often as you drink it, in remembrance of Me." For as often as you eat this bread and drink this cup, you proclaim the Lord's death till He comes.

## EXPLANATION

The Lord's Supper is an ordinance of the church. It is a symbolic reminder to believers of the sacrifice Christ made for us on the cross at Calvary.

### *ABOUT THE LORD'S SUPPER*

- **We practice an open Lord's Supper.** This means, regardless of church affiliation, we welcome anyone who has placed their faith in Christ to celebrate the Lord's Supper with us.

- **The Lord's Supper is served to individuals or families** by the Deacons of our church.

- **We serve unleavened bread.** Throughout

scripture, leaven symbolizes sin.

- **We serve unfermented wine** (grape juice). Throughout scripture fermentation represents sin.

- **Jesus was the perfect Lamb of God.** He was without sin. The bread and wine represent His body and blood, broken and spilled, to save His people from their sin.

- **We receive the Lord's Supper together.** His sacrifice unites our hearts as one.

 ## Invitation

You may have questions. You may want to hear more or discuss with someone what you've experienced today. Christ's death on the cross isn't the end of the story. It can be the beginning of something transformational in you.

Many who take part in the Passion Week Experience struggle with faith. You may be uncertain of what you believe. You may doubt the authority of scripture or the story of Jesus. *We welcome your questions and would love to explore the answers with you.*

In the next location, you will have an opportunity to ask questions. You will hear more about the relevance of His sacrifice for you.

Jesus died for our sins and rose from the dead. This Sunday is Easter. We hope you will celebrate the resurrection of Jesus with us.